BELONGS TO: ____

LEARNING JAPANESE

Journal and Notebook

Made in the USA
Coppell, TX
18 January 2022

71836868R00070